JOURNEY TO THE

Light

JOURNEY TO THE
Light
Spirituality As We Mature

edited by Ann Finch

New City Press

Published in the United States by New City Press
202 Cardinal Rd., Hyde Park, New York 12538
©1996 New City, London, Great Britain

Cover design by Nick Cianfarani
Illustrations by Duncan Harper

Library of Congress Cataloging-in-Publication Data:

Journey to the light : spirituality as we mature / edited by Ann
    Finch.

    Includes index.
    ISBN 1-56548-078-3 : $8.95
    1. Aged—Religious life—Meditations. 2. Death—Religious
    aspects—Christianity—Meditations. I. Finch, Ann.
    BV4580.J68   1993
    248.8'5—dc20   92-42032

1st printing: January 1993
2d printing: October 1996

Printed in the United States of America

Contents

Hindrances that Help

The End of the Journey

Food for the Way

Introduction

There is nothing new in describing life as a journey; but journeys are of different kinds. For some the road of life is from nothingness into nothingness: the child is born, grows, works, raises a family, and finally slips down the slope of loss and death. Others seem to be aware from their earliest days that they come from God who is their home and, in their eagerness to return, they strive to discard the apparently worthless world as soon as possible. This anthology, however, is about another route. It is the way of the pilgrim, in which the losses and pains of life are fully accepted and the beauties of this world are welcomed as messengers of the light to which the pilgrim travels. Everything, in fact, is a step on the way, and nothing more so than those things which so often seem to be set-backs.

No one suggests that the way is easy, but the conviction underlying all the pieces selected in the present work is that it has a purpose. Beyond the traumas and trials, behind the joys and delights, life leads to a meeting, a meeting with one who is infinite love. He is the light awaiting us at the end of our days.

The challenge of growing older, however, does not simply look ahead to the end of the journey. It is a matter of growth and development in the here and now, which means living our present life to the very full. The fullness now prepares us for the fullness later. We plunge into life now to plunge into a greater life later. But to live like this, we need all the help we can get, and never more so than in our journey's later stages, which, despite the very intense beauty that can sometimes be glimpsed in them, are often difficult. The discoveries of those who have travelled the same way are therefore extremely useful, and this anthology seeks to make some of their riches available.

Lawrence Freeman has described a common crisis point: "There is an elusive moment in every journey—the psychological midpoint—when we have really left where we have come from and have begun to arrive at where we are going. It is a turning point of our identity when we briefly glimpse the liberty of our spirit, although that can deeply disturb us. We see that we cannot be ultimately identified with or attached to anything that is transient."

This is the point at which the anthology takes up the journey, a journey on three levels: physical, psychological and spiritual. Growing older is a time of physical decline, bringing with it various ills and, eventually, death. If youthful ambitions have not been fulfilled it is now too late; if the ladder of success has been climbed, all too often it is found, in the words of Joseph Campbell, that "it is up against the wrong wall." What now? What is the purpose of life? All that has been labored for must now be lost. In the midst of searching questions, a turning point has been reached; it is the hour of opportunity.

No one can escape trials and suffering, but the examples of great souls show us how willing acceptance can transform them into something positive and valuable. As worldly preoccupations and pleasures weaken their hold, we are freed to seek that which is unchanging and to travel unencumbered to the light at the end of our journeying. While bodily and mentally there may be a decline, spiritually there is growth. Indeed, so far as the painful side of growth is concerned, this is not merely a personal matter, for everyone young or old can make a great contribution to the world at the exact point when they may seem most useless. As Teilhard de Chardin put it, suffering is potential energy: "If all the sick people in the world were simultaneously to turn their sufferings into a single shared longing for the speedy completion of the kingdom of God, what a vast leap toward God the world would thereby make!" An aim of this book, then, is to plot the upward curve of the spiritual life through the words of those who have been able to penetrate more deeply into the heart of the mystery.

The aging process, of course, is not merely a wearisome stripping away of everything, as many people experience that age brings peace and a wider perspective on life in which they no longer feel the need to compete or struggle to affirm their egos. This change in attitude acquired over the years means that the older person can also enjoy life and its brief beauties and pleasures more fully than before; enjoyment is not clouded by the myriad anxieties that can afflict the younger person. In the way of the pilgrim this wise tranquillity is a priceless attribute, because it is a fundamentally healthy attitude in which all the passing things of our daily existence can quietly be let go. In the preparation for paradise, in which in fact the whole of an individual's life is engaged, this capacity to appreciate the world coincides with the capacity to leave it behind.

Taken in this more complete meaning, as a full life in preparation for a fuller life, maturity is not always a question of years. Indeed, the young can be spiritually more mature than their elders and, in reality, many of the challenges faced by people growing older are faced also by those who are advancing along the spiritual path. One result of this is that often advice relevant to people who are older in years speaks also to those who are older in terms of the spirit. The same detachment, the loss of the inessential, the paring away of all the tricks of the ego, are necessary. They too need constantly to start again and to be able to face the inevitable sufferings.

Many of the pieces in this book may be familiar—old friends are always a comfort and an encouragement.

Many others may be unknown. Among these are extracts from the works of Igino Giordani, writer, politician and one-time member of the Italian parliament. No apology is made for the number of extracts included; he deserves to be better known and his writings convey a deep experience of what aging means: in fact, he would often say that only one thing is forbidden—to get old. And he meant what he said! He lived out his Christian ideals in possibly the most difficult field of all, and was a living example of charity in adversity. "A political opponent," he said, "is your neighbor to be loved." The same spiritual dynamism characterizes all his writings.

The book is divided into five parts which emphasize its character as a companion for our journey. One can go to the section necessary to find the help needed to suit one's condition, a search that should be made easier by the various titles and headings. Of course, it is also true that anyone can simply pick the book up and dip into it; in all probability they will find something useful, something brimming over with a wisdom that will help in their own, personal journey to the light.

Ann Finch

The Journey of Life

growing to maturity

The Soul Is Ageless

The human soul does not know age.

Christians grow old
but their souls do not grow old.
They draw closer to that which follows this life.
There, no one is too young, and no one is too old.

Gregory Nazianzen

Whenever I see an aged priest or brother I knew in his youth or midlife, I'm struck by the sense that this person, though now old, is living the same life he lived thirty years ago. Outside the monastery people go through significant external changes. They succeed or they fail. They do things that give them a clear history, while the monk appears to live in an eternal present.

It's as though the timeless soul experience of the monk pours out onto his life and person, while most of us show only the metamorphoses of time.

Thomas Moore

Growing Old with Grace

To grow old gracefully is a victory of the soul over the body.

The secret of growing old and at the same time remaining young lies in always being available to someone, always having something to do. He who loves never grows old.

Do not become negligent. By keeping body, spirit and soul in good shape we remain less dependent on others.

Face those difficulties which cannot be overcome or avoided with courage and without complaint. If we sacrifice them wholeheartedly to God they can be of use to the kingdom of God: they represent a valuable treasure.

We need always to remember that others are worse off than we are. The best way to alleviate our own pain is to take upon ourselves the burden of others.

Each day consider the countless small things that we can do. Give thanks for the ability to move, hear, make conversation, serve, smile, forgive, pray.

Keep all harmful things at bay: idleness, egoism, cutting yourself off from others, ill-will, jealousy, envy.

Do not lament over past joys. Be glad that they existed and thank God who gave them.

Do not live in the past or future. Live the present moment fully. It is always new and full of hope.

Do not impose on others or withdraw from them, but remain available for tasks which you can still undertake.

Join in everything which is offered to older people: for them and with them.

Show especial love toward the young. Take an interest in their future, ask them about their ideas, take part in their lives, remembering the joys and aspirations of your own youth.

When we can no longer offer the young our enthusiasm let us give them our trust. Let us become the instruments of harmony and of understanding: that is a great task.

Experience old age with all it entails. Practice its peculiar virtues: wisdom, benevolence, goodness, patience, calm, peace.

Nurture the conviction that growing old is a gift from God, a grace which allows us to participate more and more in the redeeming work of the Savior. Take comfort and joy from this.

That which keeps our spirit young is faith;
That which keeps our heart young is love;
That which keeps our will young is hope;
That which keeps our life young is Christ;
For He is the Way, the Truth, and the Life.

Do not worry unnecessarily. God takes care of the most important thing: Love. Love will never desert us.

Old age frees us from worldly affairs and it is time to think of what is to come.

Prepare yourself in peace and faith for the new life. There a Father awaits us, a Son has prepared a place for us, and a Mother will receive us. There we shall be re-united with all our loved ones.

Principles of the French Movement for the Third Age

Keeping One's Perspective

In my work as a deaconess and doctor I have found that many of us who are older brood about things that have happened to us and that we have caused to happen to other people. We find ourselves hurt by what other people have done to us in the past. It seems almost impossible to forgive them. At the same time we know that we, too, often have cause to regret something we have thought or done which has caused someone else harm. Sometimes we have been able to put things right. Sometimes we cannot redress the harm we have done: then we have to live with the consequences of our thoughts, words and actions. As we grow older and have more time for reflection, many of us, I believe, will find ourselves thinking about the past. Our thoughts will challenge us to come to terms with our failures and scars.

One of the greatest pains which may afflict us as we grow older may come from a missed opportunity to be reconciled with a parent, relative or friend whom we have hurt or who has hurt us at some time in the past.

I have a vivid memory of a small incident that happened when my mother was dying of cancer and I was nursing her. A few days before she died she was in a lot of pain and had to call for my help repeatedly. On one of these occasions she told me off, just as if I was a small girl again. I reacted with a sulky silence. The moment passed but neither of us had said "Sorry." As I got into bed I remembered that small incident. "I'll make it up in the morning," I thought, "and I'll ask the doctor to call and see if we can ease her pain more." I fell asleep quite happily.

When I went to see my mother early next morning she had slipped into unconsciousness. The incident had been trivial: at a time of grief, however, it assumed a disproportionate significance and I reproached myself bitterly for my failure to ask her forgiveness. Moreover to my horror I found that I wanted her to regain consciousness so that I could get things straight between us. Mercifully for her, that did not happen and she died peacefully three days later.

I can now see the whole of that period in proportion and I know that such a small unhealed hurt could not mar our strong love for each other. But at the time my grief was increased by remorse, not only for the immediate pain I had caused her but also for all the suffering we had inflicted on each other during my growing years. My wise husband helped me through this painful experience and waited patiently for me to recover my perspective. It took time, but in the end I found myself healed.

Una Kroll

Growing in Beauty

But where is the greatest beauty in God's eyes? Would it be in the baby that looks at you with very lively, innocent eyes, quite similar to unclouded nature? Or would it be the young girl who sparkles like the freshness of a blossoming flower? Or would it be the withered, old man, bent-over by now, almost incapable of anything, perhaps just waiting for death?

The grain of wheat is so promising when it is thinner than a blade of grass. It is bunched with the other grains, encircling and comprising the wheat head. It is waiting to ripen and get free, alone and independent, either in the farmer's hand or in the earth's bosom. It is beautiful, full of hope.

But it is also beautiful when it is ripe. By now, it is better than the others, and so it is chosen to be put in the ground in order to give life to other wheat plants. By now, it contains life in itself. It is beautiful. It is the one that has been chosen for future generations of crops.

But when it is buried, shriveling up, it compresses its being into very little. It is more concentrated and it dies slowly, decomposing in order to give life to a little plant. This plant is different from the seed, but it receives its life from the seed. Maybe the seed is more beautiful in this stage.

Different kinds of beauty.

And yet each is more beautiful than the other.

The last one is the most beautiful.

Does God see things in this way?

Those wrinkles that crease the little old woman's forehead, that shaking and bent-over way of walking, those short words full of experience and wisdom, that gentle gaze of a girl and woman together—but better than either of them . . . *This is a beauty which we do not know.*

This is the grain of wheat, dying out, which is about to start up a new life. Such a life is different from before. It is in new heavens.

I think that God sees things this way. The approach to heaven is far more attractive than the various steps along the path of life. Ultimately, this path is only needed to open that door.

Chiara Lubich
(b. 1920)

The Beauty of Age

As the clear light is upon the holy candlestick,
so is the beauty of the face in ripe age.

Ecclesiasticus 26:17

* * *

Not spring nor summer beauty
Hath such grace
As I have seen in one
Autumnal face.

John Donne

* * *

Every age has its own beauty. Why be afraid of
physical decline when the years bring deeper
insight and greater gentleness of action?

Brother Roger Schütz
Taizé

* * *

Grey hair is a crown of glory: when it is won by
a virtuous life.

Proverbs 16:31

In Youth We Prepare for Aging

Only very few people realize that it is in the days of our youth that we prepare ourselves for old age. This is an imperative we must be conscious of even in youth. Prepare spiritually for old age and learn how to cultivate it. It is an age of great spiritual opportunities, the age of completion rather than decay. The ancient equation of old age and wisdom is far from being a misconception.

However, age is no guarantee for wisdom. A Hebrew proverb maintains: "A wise old man----the older he gets the wiser he becomes: a vulgar old man----the older he gets the less wise he becomes." People are anxious to save up financial means for old age: they should also be anxious to prepare a spiritual income for old age. That ancient principle: "listen to the voice of the old": becomes meaningless when the old have nothing meaningful to say. Wisdom, maturity, tranquillity, do not come all of a sudden when we retire from business. Lectures ought to be offered in schools about the virtues that come to fruition in old age and about the wisdom and peace that arrive with it.

Abraham J. Heschel

Preparation for Aging

Old age seizes upon most men while they still retain the minds of boys, doing actions from principles of great folly and a mighty ignorance, admiring things useless and hurtful and filling up all the dimensions of their abode with business of empty affairs. They cannot pray because they are busy and because they are passionate. They cannot communicate because they have quarrels and intrigues of perplexed causes, complicated hostilities, and things of the world. And therefore they cannot attend to the things of God, little considering that they must find a time to die in. When death comes they must be at leisure for that. Such men are like sailors loosing from a port and tossed immediately with a perpetual tempest, lasting till their cordage crack, and either they sink or return back to the same place. They did not make a voyage, though they were long at sea.

Jeremy Taylor

Inner Stillness

Very old people have an inner stillness. They have a dignity which derives, not from their achievements, but from their being. In their essence we find ourselves in the presence of something which can be described as a different image of eternity.

* * *

It is incumbent upon the elderly to strengthen their sense of self-discipline, order, and consideration for others. Each time an older person feels tempted to relax self-discipline and conventional behavior, to exploit the freedom that old age affords and allows himself to do things which would previously have been frowned upon he must remind himself that he is thereby paving the way for a neglect which would disfigure his last years.

Romano Guardini
(1885--1968)

Successful Aging

To be merciful implies above all being able to listen. An experienced person who knows how to listen is especially capable of loving young people. He can help them better than others can, because he understands them better, and he understands them better because he loves them, and because his love springs from goodness. The feeling for God and for life does not automatically increase with age. Throughout his whole life man must do battle with himself and strive for perfection. He must fall in with the plan which God wishes to realize in him. Otherwise old age will lead to self-love and hypersensitivity. He who succeeds in accepting the privations and renunciations of life as an act of God matures in his faith in God. For him each restriction becomes a victory of the spirit, a transformation into a new life. As St Paul puts it, he receives a new robe. We must learn to love everything on earth, for it is love alone that will not wither. It transcends death and enters into the new state of being to which God beckons us.

Germain Barbier

The Value of Older People

We imagine that life consists of
Continual hurry and never losing
one moment.
How salutary old people are for us!
They know how the world goes.
How precious they are!
They teach us the true value of things:
Old people no longer have illusions;
They see in greater depth;
They penetrate the outward appearance of things
And sense their inner worth.

Phil Bosmans

Beauty Returned to Beauty's Giver

Come then, your ways and airs and looks, locks,
    maiden gear, gallantry and gaiety and grace,
Winning ways, airs innocent, maiden manners,
    sweet looks, loose locks, long locks, lovelocks,
    gay gear, going gallant, girlgrace—
Resign them, sign them, seal them, motion them
    with breath,
And with sighs soaring, soaring sighs deliver
Them; beauty-in-the-ghost deliver it, early, now,
    long before death
Give beauty back, beauty, beauty, beauty back
    to God,
    beauty's self and beauty's giver.
See; not a hair is, not an eyelash, not the least lash
    lost; every hair
Is, hair of the head, numbered.

Gerard Manley Hopkins

Leaving All for God

Already now my life has run its course
Through crashing seas that tossed its
        fragile boat
To that common haven where I must give
Account of all my works devout or sad.
And I can see the once fond fantasy
That made of art my idol and my king
Is merely error's cargo, borne by all
Despite the good intentions each may have.
The loving thoughts so happy and so vain
Are finished now: the double death draws near?
The one I know is sure, the other threatens.
And neither brush nor chisel can still calm
My soul. It turns to God's wide open love
Which gathers all into the cross's arms.

Michelangelo

As Age Advances, the Soul Opens to the Divine

As the days and the years glide past us like a swiftly flowing stream, we begin to feel that we are becoming more like children and the past becomes more real than the present.

Let us pray God that we may become more and more child-like by His Grace.

But as the earthly windows of sense and feeling and the earthly doorways of action close, the portals of the soul open more and more widely. Indeed a new window seems to be opened within us. The division between the Temporal and the Eternal becomes increasingly thin. It seems as if, at last, the warm sun had dispelled the mists in which the vales of life had been wrapped and shrouded hitherto, so that when the final call comes it is just stepping from this world into the Life Beyond.

Evelyn Sturge

Life Is a Process of Ripening

I feel that I have arrived at the autumn of life. The last fruits have been gathered and eaten, the last leaves have been blown away by cold gusts of wind. I am well aware of it. My inward youthfulness resists, as if fortified by trials. This lack of affections and satisfactions coming from other people has tempered it, sharpened it, as it were, made it a prow that advances toward the Mystery, so that the plant seems to gather itself together to bear fruit again in eternity.

I have endeavored for decades, without ever growing discouraged but ever starting afresh at the beginning, to give myself to persons and to institutions, to ideals, and to services: and it seemed to me that I was giving myself—as though consecrating myself without counting the cost—joyfully. Now it seems, as I look back on it, that I sowed failures to reap a harvest of ingratitude, as if persons and things, one after the other, had exploited and deceived me. They have all taken: few or none have given.

I understand; and I am not surprised. The mistake is to look for a return from man, whereas it comes from God. And God has not disappointed me. He feeds my heart daily with a youthful love, one ready to begin again from the start. Have I not written several times that when one serves one's brother, one serves the Father? One loves God by loving one's neighbor.

Experience bears out the lesson, which is this:

things and persons are to be loved, not for their own sake, and still less for my sake, but for the sake of God. And God gives the hundredfold in this life and beatitude in the next. That is what God is doing.

The fruit and the leaves fall, but from their decayed substance flowers a new Spring. In the solitude which is taking over in preparation for winter, God stands out: he is drawing near and my relationship with him is becoming more intimate and more immediate. To the extent that it loses in the human economy, it is gaining in the divine economy. Creatures detach themselves in order that I may become attached to the Creator. I fail to find love, in order that I may find Love.

The season will come to an end: action will end together with the reactions of human beings when at last I will be with God. In him there is no more history. History is a record of time, a list, as it were, of those who have died. In eternity there is pure life and it is full because it is lived in unity with God. And God is beyond time, with its seasons and their fruit and their leaves.

Seen thus, existence is a tree that grows toward heaven to flower in eternity. Seasons and disasters, disappointments and sufferings, are the prunings. The tree grows beneath a rain of bitter water—weeping is the water and the sun—to be cleansed thereby until it becomes a pure trunk rising from earth to heaven.

Life is only a process of ripening through the purification that suffering brings about in it. When it is ripe, God transplants the tree into Paradise and he gathers the fruit.

Igino Giordani (1894--1980)

Pilgrims on the Way

sharing the secrets of our fellow travellers

A Taste for What You Will Be

Being an acorn is to have a taste
for being an oak tree.

Thomas Merton

The Pilgrim

Who would true valor see
    let him come hither,
One here will constant be
    come wind, come weather.
There's no discouragement
Shall make him once relent
His first avowed intent
    to be a pilgrim.

Who so beset him round
    with dismal stories
Do but themselves confound;
    his strength the more is.
No lion can him fright;
He'll with a giant fight;
But he will have a right
    to be a pilgrim.

Hobgoblin nor foul fiend
    can daunt his spirit.
He knows he at the end
    shall life inherit.
Then fancies fly away;
He'll not fear what men say;
He'll labor night and day
    to be a pilgrim.

John Bunyan

The Shepherd Boy's Song

He that is down need fear no fall,
He that is low, no pride;
He that is humble ever shall
Have God to be his guide.

I am content with what I have
Little be it or much;
And, Lord, contentment still I crave,
Because thou savest such.

Fullness to such a burden is
That go on pilgrimage;
Here little, and hereafter bliss
Is best from age to age.

John Bunyan

Never Too Old to Start Again

I am a widower with seven children and fourteen grandchildren. By profession I am a bookseller. It seems strange, but in spite of my seventy years I do not feel old. In fact I feel that my life only began two years ago.

Let me explain. I came into the world in 1894, a member of a Catholic family. Until I was called up to join the army when war broke out, I worked on the railways. My wife, a pianist, who died in 1960, and I together tried to give our children a Christian upbringing. In the eyes of those around me I probably counted as a "good Christian," but faith became more and more an oppressive burden. In order to keep our large family I had to work hard in our bookshop in Ghent. Bad luck, illness and setbacks in business followed one after the other. But the thing that really weighed me down was the suffering of my children which cost me many a sleepless night but at which I often felt a helpless bystander.

In 1963 when I was almost seventy, my life took an unexpected turn. My son Hermann showed me a life of faith which I had never known and which I had thought to be impossible. I remember how confused I was when he and his new friends talked about suffering being, for a Christian, a means of loving others better. I thought about it for a long time. The prison in which I had enclosed myself seemed to be growing ever narrower: my scale of values was turned upside down. I began to give God the right place in my life, that is, the first place. It felt as if my soul had been equipped with an antenna. A new world erupted in me: it was like starting a new life. That is why I calculate my age from that moment on.

From his diary
Whoever does not love, goes backwards. We must always start again from the beginning.

(After a heart attack) God opened the door of my life by a hand's breadth. He showed his face for a moment and gave me a sign. Then he closed the door again. This hurt me a lot . . . but I must say that God has a sense of humor!

I used to be a pessimist, and with good reason. I had a hard life. Now I have become an optimist because I have found a "prism" through which I see things in a different way, namely, love. And it is available to everyone.

Life is still difficult and loving is not always easy. But I want to try afresh each day.

I thank God that he has given me the grace not to be lonely even when I am left alone in my room. I try to remain united to many people. Even though the bond is invisible because it is supernatural, it is nonetheless very real.

I believe the value of suffering lies in the way it opens our eyes to what really matters. Insignificant things fade into the background. God is the only one who can help us. Even if he doesn't take away the pain, he gives us the strength, the hope and the courage to endure.

When we are suffering we are one with all those who suffer. We are one body. When a finger is injured the whole organism helps it to heal. We too must be ready to help others. We are all on the road to Jericho: we are sick in body, soul and spirit. We need one another.

Suffering is a law of nature. The grain of wheat must die if it is to bring forth fruit. We admire the beauty of a flower; we rejoice in its fragrance. But it all springs from ugly roots hidden underground.

We carry a deep longing within us. We require something that the world cannot give—perfect love. I hope that I shall soon reach this destination.

I want to be with God, to contemplate him face to face so that I can love him undividedly. This is my desire: but may his will be done. . .

Paul Claeys

No Need to Stop Growing

Your way through life will not remain the same.
    There are years of happiness and years of
        suffering.
There are years of abundance
and years of poverty,
years of hope and of disappointment,
of building up, and of breaking down.
But God has a firm hold on you through
everything.

There are years of strength
and years of weakness,
years of certainty, years of doubt.
It is all part of life
and it is worth the effort
to live it to the end
and not give up before it is accomplished.

You need never stop growing.
A new future is always possible.
Even on the other side of death
a new existence waits for you
in the fullness of that glory
which God has prepared for you
from the beginning.

From the Rule for a New Brother

Living Life as a Gift of Love

12 February 1970

Today I became a great-grandmother. I shall probably never see my great-grandson. He lives on the other side of the world, in New Zealand. For this tiny human being who carries a little of my blood in his veins I ask today a precious gift: the gift of the grace of God. How many races and what a long history, both human and divine, come together in him! Tomorrow I shall write to him, so that some day he may read my letters and know that a woman who is his mother three times over prayed specially for him.

9 February 1973

Why is my heart still not at peace? Have I not learned time and time again that there is someone who guides me, who thinks about me, who watches over me, and whose presence is always with me? Haven't I understood that every weakness and fear, every failure and every humiliation is the shadow cast by his divine plan of light? Everything is good, everything is Love! But the Love of God is a mystery as strong as suffering and death, incomprehensible to fallen creatures. I must find beauty and joy everywhere where we are not able to see them or understand them, in the deepest abyss of our being.

14 March 1973

For years I thought of death almost as a sudden detachment. Now I see it as the acceptance of being slowly taken apart: it's not me who is dying, but material life which is leaving me. With joy I must come to understand that I am being freed from this mortal body. The pain and disgust of this decay should not upset me any more. In order to save the divine gift of life, I must lose it, accepting the loss with love. Never have I felt that I had so much to give, to speak, to write, to do. . .and yet my physical strength is slowly ebbing away, because the most precious gift to offer is life, to offer my life, myself, out of love.

Maria Luisa Brasile

In the Shadow of Eternity

From his journal

"Night is drawing nigh." How long the road is! But for all the time the journey has already taken, how you have needed every second of it in order to learn what the road passes by!

"I am being led further"—Yes, yes: but you have not been blind to the main chance.

"Thy will be done"—To let the inner take precedence over the outer, the soul over the world, wherever this may lead you. And lest a worldly good should disguise itself as a spiritual, make yourself blind to the value the life of the spirit can in fact bestow upon life in this world.

The hardest thing of all—to die *rightly*—an exam nobody is spared. And how many pass it? And you? You pray for strength to meet the test but also for leniency on the part of the Examiner.

"Night is drawing nigh."
For all that has been—Thanks!
For all that shall be—Yes!

Maturity: among other things not to hide one's strength out of fear and in consequence to live below one's best.

Goodness is something so simple: always to live for others, never to seek one's own advantage.

Your life is without foundation if in any matter you choose on your own behalf.

"Night is drawing nigh." Each day a first day: each day a life. Each morning we must hold out the chalice of our being to receive, to carry, and to give back. It must be held out empty: for the past must only be reflected in its polish, its shape, its capacity.

Maturity: among other things the unclouded happiness of the child at play who takes for granted that he is at one with his playmates.

In thy wind—in thy light—how insignificant is everything else! How small are we! And how happy in that which alone is great! So shall the world be created each morning anew—*forgiven*—in thee and by thee.

Dag Hammarskjold

Bid the World Goodnight

He was nearing sixty. That very day his secretary had said to him, "I wouldn't like to live to be fifty." She expressed the sentiment with the hushed awe of a person who is aghast at a possible but awful fate. She had paid him a compliment unconsciously because, sensitive girl though she was, she must not have adverted to his age. Did this mean that he didn't appear to be as old as he really was?

He was listening to a concert on his radio: Brahms' Fourth Symphony. How old was Brahms when he wrote this symphony, he wondered. Over fifty for sure! The ripe fruit of a lifetime of music-making. He went over to the book-case and took down "Music of the World." But the book gave no indication of the composer's age at the time this symphony was written.

All right, then, So I'm on the downward path, he thought. Stiffness in the joints, slowness of reactions, slight deafness. "Poor old chap," his nephews and nieces would say. "He's past it, you know. Active in his time, but now. . ."

But there was a credit side to approaching old age. He had already experienced the unexpected bonus of this time of life, the liberation from wondering (or caring about, for that matter) what sort of impression he was making on people. Of course, such unconcern had its dangers. It could imply an imperviousness to criticism, an irresponsible complacency. But once he was aware of this danger, the likelihood of self-delusion was lessened.

He had always understood that unconcern about the opinion of others was a sign of maturity. Strange to think of maturity at his time of life. Surely one should be mature much earlier in life than at nearly sixty. On the other hand one speaks about a really old wine as "mature."

I suppose I am still growing in maturity, he mused, even at my age. After all that's the purpose and end of it all. He picked up a copy of the New Testament and began to search through the letter to the Ephesians. Yes, this was the passage. "In this way," wrote Paul, "we are all come to unity in our faith and in our knowledge of the son of God, until we become the perfect Man, fully mature with the fullness of Christ himself."

"Fully mature with the fullness of Christ himself." Well, that won't be reached this side of the grave. Of that he was sure. But at least he had been consciously aiming at it over the years. He had daily tried to leave himself to the transforming power of the Spirit, having long since recognized that Heaven had written on its gates—"No immature people allowed here." So he had tried over the years to slough off the petty immaturities, stupid competitiveness, over-sensitivity to criticism, a tendency to bore people with his news and views—all these traits were, in his estimation, indications of immaturity. But there was no doubt he still had a long way to go.

He hadn't really begun seriously to think about the wrench of physical death. Not that he was afraid of it. He was even prepared to accept the indignity of it all. He often recalled his mother's death—three weeks of disintegration. "She would be kept alive for another month," the doctor said, "if you put her in a nursing home. But wouldn't you rather have her die at home with her family round her?" Well, his death would not be like that. Hardly possible for there to be any family around him. A nurse, a sister, perhaps.

He'd always hero-worshipped the Apostle Paul. And he pictured him now, in the dark dank Mammertine prison in Rome, writing pathetically to his friends, "Do your best to come and see me as soon as you can . . . only Luke is with me. When you come, bring the cloak I left with Carpus in Troas . . . and the scrolls, especially the parchment ones." But Paul knew in his heart that the end was at hand. "As for me, my life is already being poured away as a libation, and the time has come for me to be gone. I have fought the good fight to the end; I have run the race to the finish; I have kept the faith; all there is to come now is the crown of righteousness reserved for me, which the Lord, the righteous judge, will give to me on that Day; and not only to me but to all those who have longed for his Appearing" (2 Timothy).

Too early for him yet to be able to speak so confidently. But it was something for him to aim at.

The symphony ended and the audience applauded enthusiastically. Then there was silence in the room, except for the ticking of a clock and the distant hum of traffic. But the silence was more than the absence of sound. He was aware of a presence. . .

Anthony Bullen

Tasting Eternal Life

M y mother and I were alone, leaning from a window which overlooked the garden in the courtyard of the house where we were staying at Ostia. In intimate conversation we stood, "forgetting those things which are behind and reaching forth unto those things which are before" (Phil 3:13). In your presence, Lord, who are the Truth, we asked ourselves what that eternal life would be like which "eye hath not seen nor ear heard neither has it entered into the heart of man" (1 Cor 2:9).

Our conversation led us to the conclusion that even the highest joy communicated by the senses, in spite of all its splendor, always remains of a physical nature: it cannot compare with that other life. We arose with even greater longing for Existence itself. As the flame of love burned stronger in us and raised us higher toward the eternal God, our thoughts ranged over the whole compass of material things up to the heavens themselves. Higher still we climbed, thinking and speaking all the while in wonder at all that you have made. At length we came to our own souls and passed beyond them to that place of everlasting plenty where you feed Israel for ever with the food of truth. And while we spoke of the eternal Wisdom, longing for it and straining for it with all the strength of our hearts, for one fleeting instant we reached out and touched it. Then with a sigh we returned to the sound of our own speech in which each word has a beginning and ending—far, far different from your Word, our Lord, who abides in himself for ever yet never grows old, who gives new life to all things.

We told ourselves: Some day when everything falls silent, the impulses of the flesh, the pictures of the earth, of water, of air, when the canopy of heaven is at rest, and the soul no longer thinks of itself but goes beyond itself, when dreams and fantasies are silent as well as every word and sign; in short, when all is silent in a man and the creator alone is speaking—when this condition lasts and all other imaginings vanish, is it not then that that word is fulfilled which says: "Enter into the joy of thy Lord"?

This was the purport of our talk. And then my mother said: "My son, for my part I find no further pleasure in this life. What I am still to do or why I am here in this world I do not know, for I have no more to hope for on this earth. There was one reason, and one alone, why I wished to remain a little longer in this life, and that was to see you a Christian before I died. God has granted my wish and more besides, for I now see you as his servant, spurning such happiness as the world can give. What is left for me to do in this world?"

I no longer know what I replied to my mother. Some five days later she was attacked by a fever. She fainted and remained unconscious for a short while. We hurried to her side. When she recovered consciousness she looked at my brother and me as we stood by her bed and asked us, "Where was I?" When she saw our grief, she said, "You will bury your mother in this place." I said no word and it was with difficulty that I could restrain my tears. Soon afterward she said to us both, "Bury this body wherever you wish. Do not be concerned about me. All I ask of you is that, wherever you may be, you should remember me at the altar of God."

Although she hardly had the strength to speak she managed to make us understand her wishes, and then fell silent. Her illness increased in violence and so on the ninth day of her illness when she was fifty-six and I was thirty-three, her pious and devoted soul was set free from the body.

Augustine
(Bishop of Hippo, d. 430)

Light at the End

There can be no darkness without light. Do not be afraid of the darkness: there is light beyond it. If there is total darkness, then even a small light will shine out. But when the place is completely illuminated the small light appears very insignificant, almost negligible. When you feel you are lost in darkness this creates fear. But do not be afraid; because there is a light shining beyond it. Have full faith in it, that there is light: and that will remove your fear completely.

Even if you possess only a little light, that is fully capable of taking you to reach your ultimate goal. Do not be afraid that your own power is so little, so negligible. Maybe it is little. Maybe it is not illuminating the whole of your path. But whenever you move forward, it will illuminate the path immediately in front of you and as you go ahead it will provide light further ahead. There is no need to lose heart.

H. H. Shantanand Saraswati

O Come Quickly

Never weather-beaten sail more willing bent
      to shore,
Never tired pilgrim's limbs affected slumber more
Than my wearied sprite now longs to fly out of my
    troubled breast:
O come quickly, sweetest Lord, and take my soul to
    rest.

Ever blooming are the joys of Heaven's
    high paradise.
Cold age deafs not there our ears nor vapor
    dims our eyes.
Glory there the sun outshines, whose beams
    the blessed only see:
O come quickly, glorious Lord, and raise my sprite
    to thee.

Thomas Campion

The God Who Comes

During my life I have had plenty of time to discover my poverty in body, in heart, in spirit.

At first it annoyed me; sometimes it scandalized me, as something incomprehensible.

Then it made me think.

The meeting with Jesus in the gospel taught me endurance, resignation, acceptance of this poverty of mine.

But when He, Jesus, and the Father sent me the Holy Spirit, I understood and lived the beatitude of poverty—the loving and joyful understanding of my limits, the certainty that life is born of death, and the contemplative experience that visible things are images of the invisible and that poverty on this earth is only a thirst for heaven which is thirst for the Absolute.

Then I walked with faith on the path of my poverty to meet with Him, the Invisible, the Eternal One, Life, Light, Love, the Merciful One, the Personal God, the God of Abraham, the God of Moses, the God of Elijah, the God of Jacob, the God of Christ.

The meeting has not always been easy: darkness, nausea, dryness, desire to escape.

But I have remained, sustained by hope.

I have understood that God is the God who comes.

And I have waited.

For me to pray means to wait.

On the frontier of my limits, in the tension of my love, to have the strength to wait.

He always came, even if His manner of coming

was always new, because He is always new and He is eternal multiplicity, though in the infinite unity of His nature.

I tell you little when I say I have gotten on well with Him, though He has nearly always offered me a painful love, in the image and substance of Jesus crucified, and He has strongly invited me to identify my love with the sorrow of the whole world and the suffering of my brothers.

And I expect—if His grace sustains me, as I hope it will—to return every dawn and every evening of my life to that meeting place.

And even if I foresee that my poverty will grow as I approach death, and that the waiting will be always more bitter, I no longer wish to break the appointment.

By now the God who comes has conquered me, and my eyes, tired of seeing only things here below, are happy to smile at Him.

And I should like them to be well opened and ready to smile before His marvels when He comes the last time to break through the veil of my limits and to introduce me—with all "His people" which is the Church—into His invisible Kingdom of light, life and love.

In order to hurry that day, from now on I am taking for myself the most beautiful prayer, expressed in the last words of Revelation and placed like a seal on revealed things:

"Come Lord Jesus!"

How I embrace as mine the joyful hope contained in the reply: "Yes, I am coming soon."

Amen!

Carlo Carretto (1910--1988)

Hindrances that Help

suffering and loss

The Negative Disappears
in the Positive

He said not thou shalt not be tempted, thou
shalt not be travailed. But he said thou shalt not
be overcome.

Julian of Norwich

* * *

How can one get bored in life if the City of
God is there to be built up? How can one suffer
from desolation if one can live in communion with
God? How can one feel oneself alone if in solitude
above all one can converse with God? The Word
demands silence.

Igino Giordani
(1894--1980)

The Necessity of Tribulations

I am progressing along the path of my life in my ordinary contentedly fallen and godless condition, absorbed in a merry meeting with my friends for the morrow or a bit of work that tickles my vanity today, a holiday or a new book, when suddenly a stab of abdominal pain that threatens serious disease, or a headline in the newspapers that threatens us all with destruction sends this whole pack of cards tumbling down.

At first I am overwhelmed and all my little happinesses look like broken toys. Then, slowly and reluctantly, bit by bit, I try to bring myself into a frame of mind that I should be in at all times. I remind myself that these toys were never intended to possess my heart, that my true good is in another world and my only real treasure is Christ. And perhaps by God's grace I succeed, and for a day or two become a creature consciously dependent on God and drawing its strength from the right sources.

But the moment the threat is withdrawn, my whole nature leaps back to the toys. I am ever anxious, God forgive me, to banish from my mind the only thing that supported me under the threat, because it is now associated with the misery of those few days. Thus the terrible necessity of tribulation is only too clear. God has had me for but forty-eight hours, and then only by dint of taking everything else away from me. Let him but sheathe that sword for a moment and I behave like a puppy when the hated bath is over. I shake myself as dry as I can and race to re-acquire my comfortable dirtiness, if not in the nearest manure heap, at least in the nearest flower bed.

And that is why tribulations cannot cease until God either sees us remade or sees that our re-making is now hopeless.

C. S. Lewis

The Benefit of Sickness

In sickness, the soul begins to dress herself for immortality. First she unties the strings of vanity. Then she draws the curtains and stops the lights from coming in and takes the pictures down, those fantastic images of self-love and gay remembrance of vain opinion and popular noises. Then she lays by all her vain reflections, beating upon her crystal-pure mirror from the fancies of strength and beauty and little decayed prettinesses of the body.

Jeremy Taylor

Teach Me to Love Loneliness

God my Father
the ranks around me are thinning.
Do not take all my old friends from me.
Keep me open to new encounters
with people with whom I can be good
and who can help me to become good.
I am afraid of being abandoned.
Teach me to love loneliness:
it is a way that leads toward you,
for I am not alone:
you are with me.

Lord, help me, now in my old age,
to think of others first:
my relations. . .
friends and benefactors. . .
my neighbors to left and right
above and below. . .
my fellow residents in the home, men and women...
my former colleagues. . .
the weak and the sick that I know about. . .
Help me to be
wherever I am needed by someone;
to listen, without switching off,
to remain patient
even when I find it difficult.

Josef Gülden

Drifting Away: a Fragment

They drift away. Ah God! they drift for ever.
I watch the stream sweep onward to the sea,
Like some old battered buoy upon a roaring river,
Round whom the tide-waifs hand—then drift
    to sea.

I watch them drift—the old familiar faces
Who fished and rode with me by stream and wold;
Till ghosts, not men, fill old beloved places
And ah! the land is rank with churchyard mold.

I watch them drift—the youthful aspirations,
Shores, landmarks, beacons, drift alike.

I watch them drift—the poets and the statesmen;
The very stream runs upward from the sea.

Yet overhead the boundless arch of heaven
Still fades to night, still blazes into day.

Ah God! my God! *Thou* wilt not drift away.

   Charles Kingsley

Friends Departed

They are all gone into the world of light!
  And I alone sit lingering here.
Their very memory is fair and bright
And my sad thoughts doth clear.

It glows and glitters in my cloudy breast,
Like stars upon some gloomy grove,
Or those faint beams in which this hill
    is drest
After the sun's remove.

I see them walking in an air of glory
Whose light doth trample on my days,
My days which are at best but dull and hoary,
Mere glimmerings and decays.

O holy Hope! and high Humility
High as the heavens above!
These are your walks and you have showed
    them me
To kindle my cold love.

Dear beauteous Death! the jewel of the Just
Shining nowhere but in the dark;
What mysteries do lie beyond thy dust,
Could man overlook that mark!

He that hath found some fledged bird's nest
    may know
At first sight if the bird be flown.

But what fair well or grove he sings in now,
That is to him unknown.

And yet as Angels in some brighter dreams
Call to the soul when man doth sleep:
So some strange thoughts transcend our wonted
    themes
And into glory peep.

If a star were confined into a tomb
Her captive flames must needs burn there;
But when the hand that lock'd her up gives room
She'll shine through all the sphere.

O Father of eternal life, and all
Created glories under Thee!
Resume Thy spirit from this world of thrall
Into true liberty.

Either disperse these mists which blot and fill
My perspective still as they pass;
Or else remove me hence unto that hill
Where I shall need no glass.

Henry Vaughan
(c. 1621--1695)

All Stripped Away:
Alone with God

You can stay on your feet even if everyone abandons you: it is enough to lean on the Cross. The Cross keeps you on your feet and leaning against it you find yourself suddenly side by side with so many others whom the Cross supports—unfortunate creatures and saints, rich and poor, young and old, the living and the dead. You find yourself, around Christ, incorporated in the universal Church, taken up into solidarity with the angels and saints, welcomed into the arms of God.

This is not an ascent of the years: it is an ascent toward God. To grow old is to come closer to him, a growth toward his eternity, a liberation of self for his youth.

In this ascent conversation becomes dialogue: talking with men blossoms into talking with God. For he alone remains, and face to face with him, the soul, *solus cum sola.* Illnesses create silence around one: the years thin one's friends: the world falls away like a withered fruit. The very souls, who loved us in God, plan to meet us outside this world in him. Existence unfolds like a clearance operation of all that is human in order to prepare us as clean stones to build up Christ. The soul itself while it loses everything yearns to lose even itself, in order that it may give room to him.

In this development the significance of history is grasped: a process of liberation from the fleeting for the love of the Eternal: a collaboration of nature and of man with the redemption. Mortification, disappointments, betrayals, illness, desertion. . .are the pruning of the tree for the new spring which will produce flowers in heaven. Thus history is sacred history: the return journey of individuals and of society from exile to the homeland. Thus life is like a corridor which gradually becomes dark and silent, and at the end of it he who waits—Love which would have the soul, the bride, for itself.

There is no need to seek out solitude. It is enough to accept the solitude that society creates around us, abandoning ourselves on the threshold of the temple in which God is waiting. Alone with God! There we are with life.

Igino Giordani
(1894--1980)

In God There Is No Need to Fear

Do not look forward to the changes and chances of this life in fear. Rather look to them with full hope that as they arise, God, whose you are, will deliver you out of them. He has kept you hitherto. Do you but hold fast to his dear hand, and he will lead you safely through all things; and when you cannot stand, he will bear you in his arms. What need you fear, my child, remembering that thou art God's and that he has said: "All things work together for good to them that love him." Do not look forward to what may happen tomorrow. The same everlasting Father who cares for you today will take care of you tomorrow and every day. Either he will shield you from suffering or he will give you unfailing strength to bear it. Be at peace then, put aside all anxious thoughts and imaginations, and say continually: "The Lord is my strength and my shield: my heart has trusted in him and I am helped." He is not only with me but in me; and I in him.

Francis de Sales

Fear Put to Flight

Now when Christian was got to the top of the hill, there came two men running to meet him amain; the name of the one was Timorous, and of the other, Mistrust; to whom Christian said, Sirs, what is the matter you run the wrong way? Timorous answered that they were going to the City of Zion, and had got up that difficult place; but, said he, the further you go, the more danger we meet with; wherefore we turned, and are going back again.

Yes, said Mistrust, for just before us lie a couple of lions in the way, (whether sleeping or waking we know not) and we could not think, if we came within reach, but they would presently pull us in pieces.

Then said Christian, You make me afraid, but whither shall I fly to be safe? If I go back to mine own country, that is prepared for fire and brimstone, and I shall certainly perish there. If I can get to the Celestial City, I am sure to be in safety there. I must venture: To go back is nothing but death; to go forward is fear of death, and life everlasting beyond it. I will yet go forward.

So Mistrust and Timorous ran down the hill, and Christian went on his way.

John Bunyan

The "Fear" That Casts Out Fear

Where there is charity and wisdom
there is neither fear nor ignorance.
Where there is patience and humility
there is neither anger nor worry.
Where there is poverty and joy
there is neither cupidity nor avarice.
Where there is quiet and meditation
there is neither anxiety nor distraction.
Where there is fear of the Lord to guard the house
the enemy cannot find a way to enter.

Francis of Assisi
(1181/2--1226)

* * *

Fear God and keep his commandments:
for this is the whole duty of man.

Ecclesiastes 12:13

Bearing Discomfort

If thou fliest devoutly to the wounds
and precious marks of the Lord Jesus,
thou shalt find great comfort in tribulation;
neither wilt thou much regard being despised
by men, but will easily bear up
against the accusations of detractors.

Thomas à Kempis
(1379/80--1471)

Pruning

The pruning continues. Friendships, hopes, joys, have been cut away. As a writer I am not read: as a Catholic I am not welcomed: as a politician I am disregarded. I had bound myself to a religious family and found joy in communion with Christ and in a common life with Mary. My dilettantism and my pretensions, my judgment and my inability to obey have made the connection impossible for me; and in any case it was almost severed, maintained only by slender threads. I would be inclined to level reproaches of inconsistency and ingratitude, but who will assure me that they would not arise from wounded self-love, and would not damage charity? Better to retreat into silence, the silence of winter in which, like a bare plant, existence stretches out lean arms to heaven and no longer has anything but Christ. All this love given is like all the sun of the summer that is over, the warmth of which has been banished by this cold that numbs my hands and feet, my heart and my mind. I would like to cry out, "My God, my God, why have you forsaken me?"—but I am afraid of mouthing rhetoric, I would regard myself as an actor. And then . . . And then I am aware of the inflow into my spirit of a fine and serene joy as if from a deep peace: and it is like the perfume of lilies and roses flowering in a sunken garden: and its name is Mary. She is there and at once this meditation on winter and solitude appears as mere literature to me. For in spite of everything, when she is there, poetry is accompanied by youthfulness and nostalgia by peace. I will love more than before, but without interfering, in silence, not furthering my own self but furthering God—Holy Love.

Igino Giordani
(1894--1980)

God and Suffering

Meanwhile where is God? This is one of the most disquieting symptoms. When you are happy, so happy that you have no sense of needing Him, so happy that you are tempted to feel His claims upon you as an interruption, if you remember yourself and turn to Him with gratitude and praise, you will be—or so it feels—welcomed with open arms. But go to Him when your need is desperate when all other help is vain and what do you find? A door slammed in your face and a sound of bolting and double bolting on the inside. After that, silence. You may as well turn away. The longer you wait the more emphatic the silence will become. There are no lights in the window. It might be an empty house. Was it ever inhabited? It seemed so once. And that seeming was as strong as this. What can this mean? Why is He so present a commander in our time of prosperity and so very absent a helper in time of trouble?

I tried to put some of these thoughts to C this afternoon. He reminded me that the same thing seems to have happened to Christ. "Why hast thou forsaken me?" I know. Does that make it easier to understand?

Of course it's easy enough to say that God seems absent at our greatest need because He *is* absent: non-existent. But then why does He seem so present when, to put it quite frankly, we don't ask for Him?

* * *

Feelings—and feelings—and feelings. Let me try thinking instead. From the rational point of view what new factor has H's death introduced into the problem of the universe? What grounds has it given me for doubting all that I believe? I knew already that these things, and worse, happened daily. I would have said that I had taken them into account. I had been warned—I had warned myself—not to reckon on worldly happiness. We were even promised sufferings. They were part of the programme. We were even told: "Blessed are they that mourn!" and I accepted it. I've got nothing that I hadn't bargained for. Of course it is difficult when the thing happens to oneself, not to others; and in reality, not in imagination. Yes. But should it, for a sane man, make quite such a difference as this? No. And would it for a man whose faith had been a real faith and whose concern for other people's sorrows had been a real concern? The case is too plain. If my house has collapsed at one blow, that is because it was a house of cards. The faith which "took these things into account" was not faith but imagination. The taking them into account was not real sympathy. If I had really cared as I thought I did about the sorrows of the world I should not have been so overwhelmed when my own sorrow came. It has been an imaginary faith, playing with innocuous counters labelled "illness" "pain" "death" and "loneliness." I thought I trusted the rope until it mattered whether it would bear me. Now it matters, and I find I didn't.

    C. S. Lewis

Suffering as Potential Energy

Human suffering, the sum total of suffering poured out at each moment over the whole earth, is like an immeasurable ocean. But what makes up this immensity? Is it blackness? emptiness? barren wastes? No indeed. It is potential *energy.* Suffering holds hidden within it, in extreme intensity, the ascensional force of the world. The whole point is to set this force free by making it conscious of what it signifies and of what it is capable. For if all the sick people in the world were simultaneously to turn their sufferings into a single shared longing for the speedy completion of the kingdom of God, what a vast leap toward God the world would thereby make! If all those who suffer in the world were to unite their sufferings so that the pain of the world should become one single grand act of consciousness of sublimation, of unification, would not this be one of the most exalted forms in which the mysterious work of creation could be manifested to our eyes?

Teilhard de Chardin

Suffering Is a Gift

I wonder what the world would be like
if there were not innocent people
making reparation for us all?

Today the passion of Christ
is being relived
in the lives of those who suffer.
To accept that suffering
is a gift from God.

Suffering is not a punishment.
God does not punish.
Suffering is a gift—
though, like all gifts,
it depends on how we receive it.
And that is why we need a pure heart—
to see the hand of God,
to feel the love of God
to recognize the gift of God
in our suffering.

Suffering is not a punishment.
Jesus does not punish.
Suffering is a sign—
a sign that we have come so close
to Jesus on the cross
that he can kiss us,
show that he is in love with us,
by giving us an opportunity to share
in his passion.

In our Home for the Dying it is so beautiful to see
    people who are joyful
    people who are lovable
    people who are at peace
    in spite of terrible suffering.
Suffering is not a punishment, not a fruit of sin,
    it is a gift of God.
He allows us to share in his suffering
    and to make up for the sins of the world.

    Mother Teresa of Calcutta

The End of the Journey

death and resurrection

The Experience of Death

A doctor who has been long in practice knows much about death and about the "act of dying," He cannot fail to have thought long and seriously about these matters. He realizes how widespread the fear of death is, and how powerfully it affects people, even when they were not aware that they are afraid of death.

It has long seemed to me that this fear is often exaggerated. Moreover there are two distinct and different "fears" mixed together in the minds of most people. First there is the natural fear of the "act of dying," the fear that death itself will be painful, uncomfortable, distressing and terrifying. Second, there is a deeper dread (often unrecognized and unadmitted) that after death the "self" will be extinguished like a candle is puffed out, leaving dense darkness behind it.

For my part I am convinced that if we face the first and physical element in this fear, we shall have little difficulty in coming to terms with the spiritual element in it. Until we have faced the physical element we are usually unable to deal satisfactorily with the deeper spiritual dread. The fact is that the fear of the act of dying tends to blind people to many clear and evident signs that prove they are eternal. However that may be, it will be admitted that it would be a good thing to relieve as many minds as possible of the usually needless fear of the act of dying.

One thing is certain: no one is "conscious" when

he dies, although he may be conscious that he is about to die. Are we ever conscious of the act of falling asleep? At one moment we "are sleepy," at the next we are either dreaming or actually awake again.

As I have watched at hundreds of bedsides, it has been made clear to me that the "spirit"—the essential self—"falls asleep" and separates itself from the physical body *before that body dies.* Like a clock that is running down, the pendulum—the body—continues to swing for a while after the mechanism of the clock has ceased to be worked.

That is not to say that I have not witnessed distressing bedside scenes. It is, however, the watchers by the bedside who suffer most of the agonies. I admit also that I have known instances when death has seemed terrible to me—especially after strong drugs have been used. On this matter two things need to be said. First, that the use of strong drugs is best avoided whenever possible. And second that (in my experience) prayer and faith immensely reduce (and often abolish) all need for these drugs, even in the most difficult cases. As a doctor I have not hesitated to use every drug that seemed necessary, but even so I feel that I can seriously maintain my two points: first, that the fear of the physical act of dying is nearly always needless fear: second, that those who trust in God are in fact not "tried beyond what they are able to endure." We should look on death, I hold, as a perfectly healthy phase of life and should try to approach it from that point of view. Exceptions do not prove a rule.

After the age of fifty-five therefore we should begin to think quietly and honestly about death and the hereafter. No doubt it is morbid to "dwell on death" but it may be much more morbid to decline to face this great issue. I should go so far as to assert that we ought to discuss death more freely among ourselves and with mature adults. Even young people—who often bear about with them a shapeless dread of death—are sometimes helped by a discussion of it just as they are helped by an occasional talk about the problems of sex.

But the great thing is surely to cultivate during middle age the aspect of our life and experience which physical death cannot possibly touch nor effect—I mean the life of the eternal spirit that is within every man.

Having faced as well as we are able the fear of the mere act of dying we must next turn our positive efforts to the development and culture of that part of our life and experience that we call "the self." Insofar as we become "real" to ourselves the spiritual dread of self-extinction after death will dissolve and vanish away. This is, I hold, a fact of experience, and not a mere theory. It happens like that to everyone in some measure and degree. What are the facts and experiences that build up this *self-awareness in the life that is eternal?* What are the aspects of experience that need special and concerned culture during middle life?

The spirit or "true self" is fed upon and lives by experiences of the good, the beautiful, and the true—in Nature and in Humanity. It is fed by, and lives in, human love and in fellowship. The entire body of Christian experience, the witness of the Saints and Christians of all ages combine to show us that insofar as we cultivate and experience the fruits of the Spirit we become not only our "real selves" but also "eternal selves." Above all, as we come to know Jesus the Christ experimentally, we grow as eternal selves.

It seems to me that the great act of self-discovery in the eternal usually dawns slowly upon our consciousness during our middle years. Occasionally this awareness comes to men and women in a sudden burst of splendid self-realization. But in general it dawns upon us in much the same way as the sun rises after a long and anxious night spent in "watching" with a loved one. On a certain day we awake and know that we are already living in measure an eternal life in the midst of Time.

Then our dread vanishes away.

Howard E. Collier

Death as a Good

Death, thou wast once an uncouth
hideous thing,
      Nothing but bones.
   The sad effect of sadder grones:
Thy mouth was open, but thou couldst not sing.

For we considered thee as at some six
      Or ten years hence,
   After the loss of life and sense,
Flesh being turned to dust—bones to sticks.

We lookt on this side of thee, shooting short;
      Where we did find
   The shells of fledge souls left behind,
Dry dust, which sheds no tears but may extort.

But since our Savior's death did put some bloud
      Into thy face;
   Thou are grown fair and full of grace,
Much in request, much sought for, as a good.

For we do now behold thee, gay and glad,
      As at dooms-day;
   When souls shall wear their new array,
And all thy bones with beauty shall be clad.

Therefore we can go die as sleep, and trust
      Half that we have
   Unto an honest faithful grave,
Making our pillows either down or dust.

George Herbert
(1593--1633)

The Prospect of Death

Death, this momentous event! All people of the same generation are on the way together. Now one falls, now another. I am still on my way, almost alone. Most of the companions of my youth are dead. So are most of my fellow students. When four years ago I returned to my native village I met only young people. Rarely, very rarely, did I meet old people from earlier days. I was thirteen when my mother died and eighteen at my father's death. A man who is well on in years sinks his roots more and more into the invisible through all those who have died and whom he has loved and loves still. To lay down your arms means to become familiar with death. When one is defenseless, when one is no longer afraid, one no longer fears even death. One says "yes" to it every day. It is a gateway. The Risen One allows us to pass from death to life. We are baptized into his death so that we can share in his resurrection. Gradually our life contracts and our baptism and death become one single reality. Life finds in death its fulfillment through the life-giving cross. Without death life would lack reality. It would be an illusion, a dream without an awakening.

I should not like to die suddenly. I would like a few weeks of illness as a preparation. Not too long or it would become a burden to others. Then death will come to meet me. I see him coming down the hill, up the stairs, and approaching along the passage. He knocks at the door of my room. I am not afraid. I have been waiting for him, and I say:

"Come in. Let us not go straightaway. You are my guest. Sit down a moment. I am ready." Then let him take me with him into the mercy of God.

All those many, many souls, where are they? We know something about their condition but nothing of their whereabouts. Are they far from us, in other words, on other planets? But why should they have to leave this earth which they loved and on which their family and friends still live, this earth which the Lord filled with his light? They are here, quite near, just out of sight, in the mercy of God. It is our fault if we cannot see them because of our limitations and our spiritual blindness.

Once I was in the church of St Nicholas which is just nearby. I thought of all the faithful who have followed one another ever since the church was built four hundred years ago. Where are they? Where are their souls? Suddenly I understood. It is here that they prayed; it is in this church that they venerated the icons and shared the bread of life. They are here in the communion of saints, in the infinite presence of Christ. In his love we are not divided, because God exists, God exists. Eternity exists. He wants to unite us all in his love. At the resurrection he will *be* all in *all.* Cruel time which consumes and kills us, and space which buffets and divides us, will exist no more. For God will be our time and our space, because he exists, he exists. This cannot be explained. It is the secret of faith, the blessed experience of faith.

Patriarch Athenagoras
(1886--1972)

Death and Resurrection

"Timor mortis conturbat me," sings the poet: the fear of death dismayeth me. And the Author to the Hebrews speaks of those who through fear of death were subject to bondage throughout their lives.

As a boy and a young man I found little echo of such fear within me. That all men die and that I was a man were propositions to which I gave notional assent; but as far as feelings and fears or expectations went it was as though I were everlasting. There is a kind of conspiracy in our modern Western culture to hide the grim fact of death away, as though it were something indecent. Perhaps the prudishness is itself a hidden compliment to the fearfulness of death and the obscenity of dying.

One can, for a time, but with less success as one grows older, avert one's face from the certainty of one's own death. But the deaths of others will keep breaking in upon our unnatural serenity. In a long corridor of the abbey of St Paul's-without-the-Walls, in Rome, they have fixed to the wall fragments of Roman inscriptions, discovered for the most part in the vicinity of the abbey. One of these, I think a pagan one, runs somewhat as follows: "Valeria aged thirteen years two months seven days: her parents mourning." Somehow the simplicity, the brevity, the unconnectedness of this cry of uncomprehending anguish from the past has moved me to actual tears. How can pure love exist along with the meaningless absurdity of extinction?

The civilized pagans of an earlier age than ours did look death in the face, and they found that its visage was monstrous. Lucretius tried the short way out. He argued that the fear of death was quite illusory fear: not because death is not a fact, but because the fear supposes in some contradictory way that we shall survive to lament our own extinction. He offers some thirty "proofs" that there is no immortality and he concludes—as though on a note of triumph—*"Nil igitur mors est ad nos neque pertinet hilum"*: Death then is nothing so far as we are concerned and has no relation to us at all. He imagines a lament over a man who has just died: "Never again will your wife and your darling children hasten to win your first kiss and pierce your heart with silent joy. Never will you enjoy prosperity nor give protection to those you love. Unhappy man! One disastrous day has taken from you everything that makes life worth while." And his reply is: "Yes: but then you will no longer have any desire for these things." In saying which, I venture to think that Lucretius missed a point. It is here, today, while love is still vigorous and sweet, that the menace of extinction aims its blow at the significance of love itself. Love claims everlastingness, not just because it is something good which we should like to prolong, but because if death is the end of everything, love cannot be itself, even today. It is all very well to tell a man to build his hopes on a foundation of absolute and unshakable despair. But love cannot be built upon such a foundation. If death is the end, then human life is absurd. But absurdity is something that can neither be lived nor escaped from—since suicide is itself an absurd affirmation of some inverted value.

Thus it is that the Christian good news—"Christ

has been raised from the dead, the first fruits of all humanity"—not only rang out like a message of hope to a beleaguered city in the world to which it was first addressed but still today challenges our attention as not just an anodyne for evanescent sorrows and childish fears, but a possible resolution of a contradiction that lies at the heart of our experience. If we were incapable of reflection, death would not worry, but only in moments of peril frighten us. It is as thinking creatures that we are fascinated and appalled and threatened by the fact of death. And it is as thinking creatures that we can, grace helping us, attain to the Easter faith. For Christ himself has died; but he has risen and "death has no more dominion over him."

B. C. Butler

Crossing the Bar

Sunset and evening Star
And one clear call for me!
And may there be no moaning at the bar
When I put out to sea.

But such a tide as moving seems asleep,
Too full for sound and foam,
When that which drew from out the
    boundless deep
Turns again home.

Twilight and evening bell
And after that the dark!
And may there be no sadness of farewell
When I embark.

For tho' from out our borne of Time and Place
The flood may bear me far,
I hope to see my pilot face to face
When I have crost the bar.

Alfred Lord Tennyson

Three Terrors Removed

Three great terrors of death has Christ removed. He has taken away its *unnaturalness.* Death had seemed an unnatural breach in an ordered progress, a sudden halt in a great advance. Death had seemed to shut the door of hope and to blast so many a promise. But Christ has shown how Death is no sudden arrest of growth, no reversal of life's ways, no check to the highest attainment, but just the next step in an ordered advance, the freeing of new capacities, the fulfillment of man's destiny.

And Christ has taken away the cloud of *mystery*—that darkened the thought of Death. The old world indeed might speak despairingly of that far land from which no traveller returned. There was a time when men might fear the mystery of the Unknown beyond the grave. But now One has returned—returned triumphant. And He says that Death is just a "going home"—home to the Father's arms. *This* land is really more strange to us than that, for *there is the abiding home for which we were eternally destined, for which we were lovingly made.*

And that last sting of Death, its *loneliness,* has been taken away by Christ, that fear which has wrung the heart of the bravest, that great dread which solemnized Pascal as he said, "I die alone." True indeed that in the weakness of Death we may lose consciousness for a while of human fellowship; but when human hands loose us angelic hands receive us, and Christ Himself guides us through the

Valley of the shadow of Death. And of the certainty of that felt companionship, how many of us have been allowed glad witness! We have marked the glow of happiness, the smile of recognition that kindles in the face of the dying, to whom the vision of angelic ministries is granted, to whom Christ makes fresh revelation of Himself.

Frederick William Drake

Preparation for Death

Such life as remains to me
shall not be anything other
than a calm and happy preparation for death.
I accept him
and await him in faith and trust.
I trust not in myself, for I am a miserable sinner,
but in the boundless mercy of the Lord,
whom I have to thank for everything
I am and have.

Pope John XXIII

Preparing for Death

Whoever is in his eighty-sixth year cannot be far from death. It is therefore up to me to make such preparations that I can die in the fullness of joy. I must make death a reality while I am still in this life: every day must be a dying of the old man (cf. Rom 8:13), a "dying to myself" by self-denial, mortification, self-conquest. And on the other hand, a "becoming acquainted with heaven," so that my true home is already in heaven (cf. Phil 3:20). Thus my earthly way must be a gathering of "treasure in heaven" (Mt 6:20). My true treasures in heaven are not the honor accorded to me by men, not my fame, not all the titles and decorations, but the works which will follow me (cf. Rv 14:13). Therefore "act with Christ and for Christ" for as long as he leaves me the strength to do so.

This is my best preparation for dying. And my dying will not be lonely. "Depart, Christian soul, may the Angels and Saints receive you," yea, even the Savior himself. Every Holy Communion shall be a refreshment along the way, so that at a sudden death I shall not die without refreshment along the way. God himself will preserve me from the Evil One and lead me into like eternal! If I live like that, I *shall* be able to die in the fullness of joy.

Cardinal Bea

Approaching Death with Calm

As one approaches death, one is greatly tempted to add up one's shortcomings, weaknesses and sins, and to lose courage. I believe it is better not to count at all, not to debate at all. "Yes, my shortcomings, weaknesses and sins are even more numerous and graver! But there is that which is even greater than my shortcomings, weaknesses and sins—the mercy of the Lord!"

Some day the sun will for each of us rise for the last time. Sister light, would it be possible to warn me when my last day dawns? But best of all is still the endeavor of the Christian to live each day as if it were the last: or better still—as if it were ever the first.

Helder Camara
(b. 1909)

Our Expectations at Death

What do you expect at the destination of your life's journey? Everything! If I had nothing to expect after death life would lose its meaning for me. I could understand neither suffering nor true love. For I can see these two realities only in the light of eternity. There can be no senseless absurd suffering. Pain is not the last word. It can only be explained as birth-pangs. Because our earthly life is in the last instance only a time of preparation and novitiate for eternity, I see—in spite of all the darkness—the shaft of light which illumines all the events of my life and clarifies them through love. This love I have always sought, and I can understand it only as a requirement of eternity because humans refuse so instinctively to love and be loved for only a limited time. True love aims at immortality. It is an appeal for the victory of life over death. The only future I wait for I see as light and clarity, as joy and fulfillment of all I longed for here below.

When Leon Bloy was dying he was asked: "What do you feel at this moment?" He replied: "Immense curiosity." I wish that my answer would be: "Immense trust in the love of God."

Cardinal Léon-Joseph Suenens
(b.1904)

A Letter to Death

Dear Brother Death,

Every day we come a little nearer to you. Every day we write a fresh page in the book of life which will one day come to an end. Others too write their pages and when they have all written their pages the book of humanity will finally be opened. It will be a precious book; for we are all recorded in it, we all belong to one family in the kingdom in which you, dear death, no longer exist. For you are a brother who in reality does not really exist here. There, is God, Jesus, life. You lead us to him. You are the gateway, the transition.

Every day has its evening. Your day will have no end: instead it will be the morning of the new life. We shall die in order not to die any more: to live eternally. We do not know when that day will be. This can worry us. But we have a brother who did not know your day either, and that brother was the Son of God: Jesus. However, would it not be even more painful if we knew everything beforehand? Would it not be more dangerous? We might love Jesus with a mixture of self-interest. We would love Jesus for the sake of transition, not so much for himself. Since we do not know that day, we have to act differently. We must love God in the way he wants to be loved, now, as if we were to die this day, as if we were to stand before him today. That is why Charles de Foucauld prayed: "Lord, grant me to live in such a way that I could die a martyr's death today."

Dear Brother Death, you must not be disappointed if we do not regard you as our life's destination. Life presses on; there is something within us that cannot die. You are the point of intersection between now and the hereafter, but eternal life has begun already. The life of heaven is already in us and already lives among us. Here it is still subject to the laws of time and space but it is not imprisoned by them. When therefore we ask ourselves how we can best prepare for the encounter with you, you point heavenward, as if to say: live here below as you will live thereafter. Let it be here on earth as it is in heaven . . . We do not know how it will be there, but we know enough to model our lives on the life of heaven. We can begin to build here now, with imperishable stones, the mansion which we are to inhabit beyond this life.

In heaven we will live in an eternal present. We can live like this here. Moment by moment we can do what God wants us to do. How often we worry about things we will not be able to do in the future! But we are accomplishing them now. So let us live now, let us love now, with all the strength that we have, now. There, all will be love. Everything passes, only love remains. so let us live in such a way that we will not regret not having loved enough. We can give everything freely to God. We can give everything to God as he appears in our brothers and sisters, especially in the poor. Then we shall have a treasure which will keep its value in the heavenly mansion, a value which nothing can destroy. Let us make a gift of everything we have, something which lasts. For in the end we shall have to leave it behind. Dear Brother, when you knock at the door we shall be able to make our final gift, our finest present, our life. In that moment we shall be as we truly want to be: we shall be love. For we do not want to give away something belonging to us: we want to give ourselves. The encounter with you will be the high point of our life, of our surrender, the last act of love containing all our love.

Dear Brother, you act as a backdrop for a meeting, a meeting with the one who created us and who has loved us infinitely. That is why we look forward to that encounter as a bride looks forward to her bridegroom.

What will that day be like? For the others it will be a day like any other: morning papers, problems great and small, hustle and bustle, traffic, world events, duties and pleasures. But for me, it will be *the* day of my life; there will not be another. How we shall die we cannot know, but we can already live as if our last hour had come; we can already speak as if the last word were being spoken; we can pray today as if it were our last conversation with God.

We can already make an offering to God of the hour of our death. We can give him our dying; we can give him the circumstances of our death, the how and the where; for we do not know whether we shall have the strength to do it when the time comes. And we can practice something important: trust. For on that day it will not be death that awaits us but a father who knows us. And he is mercy; he awaits us with the divine life of the Trinity, with the Mother of God and with all our brothers and sisters who have already found their home with him.

The first Christians did not call that day the day

of death, but their birthday. Birth into a new life is always bound up with pain, with struggle, with anxiety and stress. The grain of wheat has no joy when it surrenders to the law of life: it does the will of God. That is how we can prepare for this dying: by accepting the pain and the sickness, those small steps on the way, from the hand of God, learning to say with Jesus: "Not my will, but yours, Father." Let it be so. Dear Brother Death, this has become a long letter. I know that many people believe there can be nothing more bitter than you. Many do not want to speak to you. Life, they say, is hard enough, why have darker thoughts? That is why some of our brothers and sisters try not to admit you into their lives. They try, but they do not succeed. You have been there ever since we came into the world. You belong to life, just as the flowers bloom and then fade.

I thank you for letting me speak to you, for letting me live with you. True, you will come like a thief in the night. But I shall recognize you because you are no longer a stranger to me: you are my brother.

H. S.

The Beauty of Death

It is not death that will come for me, but God.

Thérèse of Lisieux

* * *

Death exists that we need die no more.

Sertillanges

* * *

I love death because through it
everything becomes new.

Carlo Carretto
(1910--1988)

Sister Death

Praise to thee, Lord, for our sister,
the death of the body.
From her no mortal may escape.
Woe to those who die in mortal sin!
Blessed are they who find themselves in thy most
holy will;
For the second death cannot harm them.

Francis of Assisi
(1181/2--1226)

Looking to God at Death

February 6th, 1691

My Good Mother,
God knows very well what is our need; and all he does is for our benefit. If we knew how much he loves us we would be ever ready to receive equally at his hands the sweet and the bitter. Even the most painful things and the most hard would be sweet and pleasing to us. The direst sufferings appear unbearable to us only from the point of view we hold; and when we are persuaded that it is the hand of God which deals with us, that it is a father full of love who places us in conditions of humiliation, grief, and suffering, all the bitterness is removed and they have only sweetness.

Let us give our thoughts completely to knowing God. The more one knows him the more one wants to know him: and since love is measured commonly by knowledge, then the deeper and more extensive knowledge shall be, so love will be the greater: and if love is great, we shall love him equally in suffering and consolation.

Let us not hold ourselves back by seeking or loving God in return for the favors he bestows upon us, lofty though they can be; or for those he can do for us. These favors, great though they are, will never bring us near to him as faith does by one simple act. Let us seek him often: through his virtue He is in our midst. Let us seek him nowhere else.

Are we not discourteous and guilty of ignoring him busying ourselves with a thousand trifles which displease and perhaps which offend him? He endures them all the same, but it is much to be feared that one day they may cost us dearly.

Let us begin by being his without reservation. Let us banish from our mind all that which is not himself. He wants to be the only one. Ask of him this grace. If we do on our part what we can, we shall soon see the change in us for which we hope. I cannot thank him enough for the small relief he has given you. I hope, by his mercy, for the favor of seeing him in a few days. Let us pray for one another.

I am, in our Lord,
Yours etc.

Brother Lawrence

(To the Reverend Mother of a neighboring convent shortly before his own death.)

Fear of the Unknown

Besides suffering, what I fear about death (why not admit it?) is the unknown, a change of the world or at least part of the world. The realities of faith, at least instinctively, do not have the same consistency as those of experience. Thus inevitably we are overcome by feelings of terror and vertigo. But this is how Providence wants it to be.

But that is the very moment when we must let ourselves be conquered by love, by trust, and by being part of an All which is greater than us. Death does not return us to a great complex of matter as the pantheists promise. Rather we are once more received, taken in, governed, by a divine Power.

Death delivers us back to God. He lets us come to him. So we must surrender to death with great love and devotion. For when it arrives there is nothing left for us but to let ourselves be ruled and led by God.

Teilhard de Chardin

Death, a Reason for Joy

The deepest reason for my joy lies in my readiness to leave this earthly life some day and to pass to a life that will never end. It does not greatly concern me what God's eternity will be like. I have better things to do than to try to imagine what heaven will be like. But just knowing that one day I shall be able to close my eyes in peace and go to meet Christ is a reason for joy.

Acceptance of death makes me rediscover a new vitality.

Brother Roger Schütz
(Taizé)

Former Things Are Passed Away

"Death shall be no more, nor mourning, nor crying, nor sorrow shall be any more; for the former things are passed away." Nor any more sin; nor any more guilt; nor more remorse; no more punishment, no more penitence, no more trial, no infirmity to depress us; no affection to mislead us; no passion to transport us; no sloth, no pride, no envy, no strife; but the light of God's countenance proceeding out of the throne.

John Henry Newman

Free Yourself from Fear

Dear Soul,
From what peril and fear you could free yourself if you lived in holy fear, mindful of your death. Apply yourself so as to live now that at the hour of death you may be glad and unafraid. Learn now to die to the world that you may begin to live with Christ.

Thomas à Kempis
(1379/80--1471)

Heaven—Haven

I have desired to go
Where springs not fail,
To fields where flies no sharp and sided hail
And a few lilies blow.

I have asked to be
Where no storms come,
Where the green swell
Is in the havens dumb,
And out of the swing of the sea.

Gerard Manley Hopkins

No Need to Fear Death

There is no need to fear death
  because death is nothing more than going
  home to God.
For me, that is the greatest development
  of a human life:
to die in peace with God.

We have homes for the sick and dying—destitutes—
and it is so beautiful to see how these people
who have lived such difficult lives
die with such contentment—with such peace—it
really is unbelievable.

We picked one of them out of a drain once
and brought him to the Home for the Dying.
I remember him saying:
"I have lived like an animal in the street,
but I am going to die like an angel—loved
  and cared for."
He had no fear.
We fear only when our conscience is not clear,
when we are afraid to face ourselves.
That is why so many people are afraid of death—
they are afraid of facing reality, of facing self,
by looking at God.
A pure heart sees God;
and I think the poor people live very much
  in the presence of God.
That is why they have no fear.
That is why they meet death with happiness.

I find that our people in the Homes for the Dying,
our lepers and so on,
their happiness at death
is not due to their being released from suffering.
It is because they are truly at peace—
a peace which shines through in their faces.
Although thousands of people die in our Homes
    each year,
I have never yet seen anybody die in distress
    . . . or in despair . . .
or restless . . .
they simply go home to God.

Mother Teresa of Calcutta

Golden Thoughts on Death

It is not to think black but golden thoughts that we think of death. Even among an abundance of graces, sometimes we are seized by the sense of the loneliness of exile on earth, and we find ourselves wanting to say again with Paul: "I should like to depart and be with Christ, which is a far better thing," or "We would rather leave our home in the body and go to live with the Lord."

The more we appreciate and go into the depths of suffering, the more we also understand that death is the ultimate offering of ourselves as "royal priests" here on earth and, therefore, the culmination of our lives. For whoever loves and knows what it means to love, it is the desired moment.

I would like to explain what I mean.

It is really "desired" in the sense that gold is desired and smoke is not. In short, a moment kissed by God, as Jesus crucified is kissed.

Our Christian brothers and sisters who have died and have lived the moment of death know what it is. Oh! how often we would like someone to have come and told us something about this "passing". . .

But perhaps—no certainly, because this, too, is love—it is better that each one of us should go through this unique experience in life: it has more value and . . . for the little suffering, for the little faith we have in God's love for us in those moments, then for all eternity we will be with him.

Chiara Lubich (b. 1920)

Fulfillment

Death is the fruit of a whole life.

Maximilian Kolbe

* * *

Death is not extinguishing the light,
but putting out the lamp
because the dawn has come.

Rabindranath Tagore

Food for the Way

prayers and meditations

Saint Teresa's Bookmark

Let nothing trouble you,
Let nothing scare you,
All is fleeting,
God alone is unchanging.
Patience
Everything obtains.
Who possesses God
nothing wants.
God alone suffices.

Teresa of Avila

An Older Person's Hymn of Praise

Blessed be they who show consideration for my wavering footsteps and my feeble hands.
Blessed be they who realize that I have to strain to hear all that is said.
Blessed be they who appear to know that my eyes have grown dim and my thoughts slow.
Blessed be they who linger with a friendly smile to chat with me a little while.
Blessed be they who never say, "You have already told me this story twice today."
Blessed be they who know how to awaken in me memories of time past.
Blessed be they who impart to me that I am loved and respected and not abandoned.
Blessed be they who by their kindness lighten the days that remain on my way to my eternal resting-place.

Author unknown

Prayer of the Third Age

L ord, teach me how to grow old!
Convince me that the community does me no wrong if it lifts responsibilities from my back, no longer asks my advice, and finds others to take my place.

Take from me the pride of experience and the sense of my indispensability. May I be able to accept, in this gradual detachment from things, what is simply the law of time; and may I be able to see in this change in my duties one of the most fascinating manifestations of life renewed by your Providence.

Keep me, O Lord, useful to the world, contributing by my optimism and my prayers to the joy and the courage of those who are now in the harness of responsibility; and make me humble and serene in my contact with the changing world, having no regrets for the past, offering my sufferings as a gift for the reconciliation of society. May my leaving the field of action be simple and natural, like the gentle setting of the sun.

Forgive me if only today, in tranquillity, I understand how much you have loved me and helped me. At least in this moment may I have a clear and full perception of the destiny of incredible joy you have prepared for me, and towards which you have set me walking since the very first day of my life.

Lord, teach me how to grow old like this! Amen.

Anonymous

Prayer

God rejoices if we trouble him.

The Curate of Ars

* * *

Do you know which is the most beautiful
moment of the day?
It is when you pray, because you are talking to the
one you love most.

Chiara Lubich
(b. 1920)

* * *

For a Christian in old age only one thing
can be at the core of life—prayer.

Romano Guardini
(1885--1968)

* * *

In your prayers do not seek the consolations of
God, but the God of consolations.

Francis de Sales

Enlighten Me, Lord

O Light of Light, enlighten all inward
obscurities in me, that after this life
I may never be cast into outer darkness.
Enlighten my soul, sanctify my body,
govern my affections and guide my thoughts,
that in the fastest closure of my eyelids
my spirit may see Thee.
Suffer me not, O my God,
to forget Thee in the dark.

Henry Vaughan
(c. 1621--1695)

Prayer Answered

I asked for strength that I might achieve;
He made me weak that I might obey.
I asked for health that I might do greater things;
I was given grace that I might do better things.
I asked for riches that I might be happy;
I was given poverty that I might be wise.
I asked for power that I might have the praise of
    men;
I was given weakness that I might feel the need of
    God.
I asked for all things that I might enjoy life;
I was given life that I might enjoy all things.
I received nothing that I asked for, but all that I
    hoped for;
My prayer was answered.

Anonymous

A Blessing on Our End

Lord Jesus Christ, the ending of any task leads us to you just as much as its beginning, for you are beginning and end.

This ending of ours, Lord, is but a small beginning, our mission and not its achievement, our good resolutions and not their fulfillment. But you have given us the beginning. Of you it is written: "He is faithful who has called you, who also will do it." Therefore we ask you: grant us your grace in full measure as we now try again to carry out the life and the mission you have entrusted to us.

It is the same old world which lies in wait for us, O Lord, the same as ever: our own weakness and sinfulness, the old familiar surroundings, the same daily round, the darkness of the future today as yesterday, our same consciousness of the Old Adam in us. This is why we have no faith in ourselves or our good resolutions, in our enthusiasm, or even in our strength of purpose. But we do have faith in your grace, in your forbearance and patience with us.

Only stay with us, O Lord; stay with us through the day, and when it is toward evening. We do not ask that your continuing presence should be reflected for us in lofty emotions, for these only reflect ourselves, not you. We can believe without these that you are with us all days even unto the end, when the bitter cup of your death must be drained. You are with us: that suffices.

Stay with us: this is our plea. Stay with us in your Holy Spirit; in the Spirit of the fear of God; in the

Spirit of contrition, humility and chaste fear, lest we dishonor the holiness of God by sin; in the Spirit of faith and of the love of prayer; in the Holy Spirit of courage and of responsibility for your Gospel, and for your kingdom in this world and in our time; in the Spirit of generosity and magnanimity; in the grace of the love of your holy cross. Time and again you become the holy Bread for us, pilgrims between time and eternity. Grant then that we may receive you with sincere faith and true love, you, the Lord of our lives and source of all grace, our strength in dying, our pledge of eternity, and the holy bond of love between us and your brothers and sisters. Give us the grace to recognize all that crosses the plans and calculations of our life as your cross and as a sharing in your death which reveals true life. Fill our hearts with the power of your eternal victory and with the blind trust that your kingdom will last forever and will rise victorious where we are only conscious of apparent defects.

Lord, you see that we ask but for one thing: that you will stay with us and that we may always imitate you. We ask you to give us only what you have already given us, to complete what you yourself have begun. We ask you for only one thing—you yourself. Since you are in truth the love of God incarnate we know that you hear our prayer. You gave yourself to us, you even fixed your destiny and your life in the history of the world and humanity, you became our friend and brother, the true companion of our existence and our destiny. You became like us in everything. So it does not offend you to be with us and to regard our cause as your cause. You always hear our prayer; and our prayer for your continuing presence in us is the first-fruit of your presence in us now.

To you is entrusted all that we have and are: our salvation, our vocation, our daily work, our families, our life and our death. So at the end, O Lord, our prayer is the sum of all desire and all prayer. Take and receive, O Lord, my whole freedom, my memory, my understanding, and my whole will, all that I have and possess. From you it came, O Lord: to you I offer it all again. All is yours; dispose of it entirely according to your will. Give me only your love and your grace, for that is enough. Amen.

Karl Rahner

Being Rooted in God

It is good to give thanks to the Lord, to sing praise to your name, Most High, To proclaim your kindness at dawn and your faithfulness throughout the night. For you make me glad, O Lord, by your deeds; at the works of your hand I rejoice. A senseless man knows not, nor does a fool understand this. The just man shall flourish like the palm tree, like a cedar of Lebanon shall he grow. They that are planted in the house of the Lord shall flourish in the courts of our God. They shall bear fruit even in old age; vigorous and sturdy shall they be, Declaring how just is the Lord, my Rock, in whom there is no wrong.

From Psalm 92

We Are Surrounded by Love

Almighty Father, thy love is like a great sea that girdles the earth. Out of the deep we come to float awhile upon its surface. We cannot sound its depth nor tell its greatness, only we know it never faileth. The winds that blow over us are the breathing of thy spirit, the sun that lights and warms us is thy truth. Now thou dost suffer us to sail calm seas; now thou dost buffet us with storms of trouble; on the crest of waves of sorrow thou dost raise us; but it is thy love that bears us up; in the trough of desolation thou dost sink us that we may see nought but thy love on every side. And when we pass again into the deep, the waters of thy love encompass and enfold us. The foolish call them the waters of misery and death: those who have heard the whisper of thy Spirit know them for the boundless ocean of eternal life and love.

Anonymous

Living Eternal Life Now

Lord make me an instrument of thy peace.
Where there is hatred let me sow love;
Where there is injury, pardon;
Where there is doubt, faith;
Where there is despair, hope;
Where there is darkness, light;
Where there is sorrow, joy.

O divine Master, grant that I may not so much
    seek
To be consoled as to console;
To be understood as to understand;
To be loved as to love.
For it is in giving that we receive;
It is in pardoning that we are pardoned;
It is in dying that we are born to eternal life.

Francis of Assisi
(1181/2--1226)

In You Have I Put My Trust

In you, O Lord, I take refuge; let me never be put to shame. In your justice rescue me, and deliver me; incline your ear to me, and save me. Be my rock of refuge, a stronghold to give me safety, for you are my rock and my fortress. For you are my hope, O Lord; my trust, O God, from my youth. My mouth shall be filled with your praise, with your glory day by day. Cast me not off in my old age; as my strength fails, forsake me not. O God, you have taught me from my youth, and till the present I proclaim your wondrous deeds; And now that I am old and gray, O God, forsake me not till I proclaim your strength to every generation that is to come. Your power and your justice, O God, reach to heaven. You have done great things; O God, who is like you?

From Psalm 71

We Journey toward Life

If universal history is a fifth gospel for humanity, the course of each individual's life is the same thing for him. Seen from God's point of view it appears as a plan for bringing us back from dispersion to unity with him. One sees then how detachment from the persons dear to one and the loss of honors and position are a clearance of human elements in order to launch you alone with God alone. And then every day takes on the value of a divine adventure, if it is used to make you mount along the sun's ray—your ray, the one which connects with the Sun that is God. It is spoken of as a journey toward death; and it is progress toward freedom, on the summit of which the Father awaits you; therefore a journey toward life, a life which never has an end.

Igino Giordani
(1894--1980)

Rest in God

A nd he showed me more—a little thing the size of
a hazel nut on the palm of my hand, round like
a ball. I looked at it thoughtfully and wondered,
"What is this?" And the answer came, "It is all that
is made." I marvelled that it continued to exist and
did not suddenly disintegrate, it was so small. And
again my mind supplied the answer, "It exists both
now and for ever because God loves it." In short
everything owes its existence to the love of God.

In this "little thing" I saw three truths. The first is
that God made it; the second is that God loves it;
and the third is that God sustains it. But what is he
who is in truth maker, keeper and lover I cannot tell;
for until I am essentially united with him I can never
have full rest or real happiness; in other words, until
I am so joined to him that there is absolutely nothing
between my God and me. We have got to realize the
littleness of creation and to see it for the nothing
that it is before we can love and possess God who
is uncreated. This is the reason why we have no ease
of heart or soul, for we are seeking our rest in trivial
things which cannot satisfy, and not seeking to
know God, almighty, all-wise, all-good. He is true
rest. It is his will that we should know him, and his
pleasure that we should rest in him. Nothing less
will satisfy us. No soul can rest until it is detached
from all creation. When it is deliberately so detached
for love of him who is all, then only can it experience
spiritual rest.

Julian of Norwich

How to Suffer Well

Lord Jesus, we thank you
that in our suffering
you have revealed to us the depths
of your boundless love.
You are with us in our suffering
and you give us quite undeserved comfort.
But, despite having experienced all this,
I still recoil from suffering, illness and difficulties.
Certainly there is no need for me to pray
that you should send me further suffering.
Preserve me from suffering
that exceeds my strength,
and give me strength
to say a whole-hearted "Yes"
to my part of your redemptive suffering
which you ask me to share;
and to thank you at all times
for giving creative meaning to our suffering.
Send us your Holy Spirit
so that we may experience the healing and
liberating power of life in union with you;
and that we may play our part
in lightening the suffering of others
and in helping them, the incurable,
patiently and with confidence.

Bernard Haring

True Peace of Heart

Grant me your grace, most merciful Jesus, and it may be with me and continue with me to the end.

Grant me always to will and to desire that which is most acceptable to you, and which pleases you best.

Let your will be mine and let my will always follow yours and agree perfectly with it.

Let me always will or not will the same as you; and let me not be able to will or not will anything otherwise than as you will it or will it not.

Grant that I may die to all things that are in the world and for your sake love to be despised and not to be known in this world.

Grant that I may rest in you above all things desired, and that my heart may be at peace in you.

You are the true peace of the heart; you are its only rest; out of you all things are hard and uneasy.

In this peace that is in you, the one sovereign eternal good, I will sleep and I will rest.

Thomas à Kempis
(1379/80--1471)

Self-surrender

Father,
I abandon myself into your hands;
Do with me what you will.
Whatever you may do, I thank you;
I am ready for all; I accept all.

Let only your will be done in me
And in all your creatures.
I wish no more than this, O Lord.

Into your hands I commend my soul,
I offer it to you
with all the love of my heart.
For I love you, Lord,
And so I need to give myself,
To surrender myself into your hands,
Without reserve
And with boundless confidence.
For you are my Father.

Carlo Carretto
(1910--1988)

It Will Be Heaven

From time to time I become aware of a truth so beautiful that I can only feel it as a premonition. It is too great for me to grasp. But it shakes me to the core, it touches my innermost being, it gives me courage, it makes me shout with joy.

I become aware where I am bound, that heaven has been promised me if I live as I should and fulfil the task that God has given me. This promise I believe in with all my life.

Heaven!

Do we sometimes think of it? Are we aware that this earth is not the place in which to settle more and more comfortably so as to find the most carefree existence? Here, every instance of our life is a step toward another country, another kingdom, homewards where we shall for ever experience the pure full happiness that we long for so ardently.

And what will it be like over there? Better not to waste words on this: we would only talk away the new reality with useless fantasies. But one thing we know: it will be . . . heaven!

Chiara Lubich
(b. 1920)

Acknowledgements

Thanks and acknowledgements are due to the authors and publishers mentioned below for permission to print extracts from works for which they hold the copyright: Burns and Oates Ltd. for *A Blessing on Our End* by Karl Rahner and an extract from *Bid the World Goodnight* by Anthony Bullen; Howard E. Collier, Evelyn Sturge and The Quaker Home Service for extracts from *The Glory of Growing Old;* Reverend Paul Drake for *Three Terrors Removed* by Frederick William Drake; Alfred A. Knopf, Inc. and Faber and Faber Ltd. for extracts from *Markings* by Dag Hammarskjold; Dom Charles Fitzgerald-Lombard, Abbot of Downside, for an extract from the work of Bishop B.C. Butler; Orbis Books for extracts from *The God Who Comes* by Carlo Carretto; Darton, Longmann and Todd for extracts from the *Rule for a New Brother* and two anonymous prayers from *All Is Harvest;* the Study Society for an extract from *Good Company* of the sayings of H. H. Shantinand Saraswati; Fanan, Saws and Gnoux Inc. for *In Youth We Prepare for Death* by Abraham J. Heschel; Harper Collins for an extract from *Meditations* by Thomas Moore, and *Growing Older* by Una Kroll and extracts from *The Business of Heaven* and *A Grief Observed* by C.S. Lewis.

Very special thanks are due to Verlag Neue Stadt from whom the initial idea for this volume came. In particular Neue Stadt is to be thanked for the following extracts from *Wenn Die Jahre Vergehen: The Prospect of Death* by Patriarch Athenagoras; *Successful Aging* by Germain Barbier; *Preparing for Death* by Cardinal Bea; *The Value of Older People* by Phil Bosmans; *Living Life as a Gift of Love* by Maria Brasile; *Approaching Death with Calm* by Helder Camara; *Never Too Old to Start Again* by Paul

Claeys; *The Soul Is Ageless* by Gregory Nazianzen; *Inner Stillness* and *The Attitude of Prayer* by Romano Guardini; *Teach Me to Love Loneliness* by Josef Gülden; *How to Suffer Well* by Bernard Häring; *Preparation for Death* by Pope John XXIII; *Growing Old with Grace* from the Movement for the Third Age; *Letter to Death* by H. S.; *Our Expectations at Death* by Cardinal Suenens.

For translations from the German, we express our gratitude to Elizabeth Houlton and Dorothy Kauffmann for their very hard and timely work.

Apologies are offered to any authors or publishers not mentioned, through inadvertence or our inability to trace them; this will be rectified as soon as possible.

Index of Authors